The Windkeeper

written by Emma Broch Stuart

illustrated by Jennifer Savage Britton

"The Windkeeper": Written by Emma Broch Stuart and Illustrations & Book Layout by Jennifer Savage Britton

ISBN: 978-1-936341-78-8

"[God] brings out the wind from His storehouses."

Psalm 135.7

For my son Cameron

Your "baby wind" waits for you in heaven.

The Windkeeper

DeWard™
for your journey

Wendall Windkeeper hurried toward the storehouse. Cold air nipped at his cheeks. This corner of heaven was cooler than others. He'd come outside prepared though, with his favorite purple cap. The one with ear flaps that flapped. With his hands deep inside the warm pockets of his coat, Wendall walked faster.

After months of training, today was the day. Ready to depart the storehouse was Wendall's most difficult batch of wind. He worried about those four little gusts. Would they be okay without the windkeeper's guidance once they reached Earth?

Wendall thought back to the first day God created them. The windkeeper remembered that God had stopped by the storehouse to check on their progress. He hovered nearby to watch their first training class. Wendall remembered being nervous. God didn't usually take so much interest in the winds after He created them. He just trusted the windkeeper to train them up in the way they should blow. Even in the beginning Wendall had wondered why this batch of wind was so special that God would pay a visit to the storehouse.

"All right," he had said to the newly created wind. "Just blow up there and see if together you can make the windmill turn."

The little winds blew around in every direction, tripping over one another's puffs of air. Wendall's ear flaps blew left then right. He scratched his brown whiskers. "Little winds, you must blow together as one or you won't even reach the windmill." God chuckled.

The windkeeper glanced over his shoulder. His face grew hot. How embarrassing. "Heavenly Father, I welcome your advice concerning this particular batch of wind," he had said. God smiled. His whole face shined like the sun. "They will be ready when I need them." And with that He turned and floated out of the storehouse. The windkeeper remembered his purple cap blowing off his head and landing on the floor. Wendall had slowly turned. The naughty wind gust whooshed behind his siblings, trying to hide.

The windkeeper had shaken his head, wondering how he would ever get them ready in time? And now, months later, they were as ready as they would ever be.

Wendall reached the storehouse and opened the double doors just a crack and slipped inside. No sense tempting the four winds to sneak out before God's appointed time. They were highly favored. Why? Wendall still didn't know.

The Lord kept His purpose for them hidden. But the windkeeper didn't need to know why. He just remained faithful in the work God set before him. And that meant training the winds the Lord created.

As Wendall rounded the corner, a leaf glided by his ear. He came to a halt and watched his little winds practice beside a tree. East Wind grabbed an orange leaf from mid-air and steadied it while it made circles. The windkeeper smiled. East Wind had been working on her balance and direction. Next, West Wind fluttered over, caught the leaf with his puff of air, and swirled it toward North Wind. North Wind rushed in and slammed the little leaf to the ground. Wendall's smile faded. North Wind, that naughty gust. Always charging in, never working as a team. Wendall shook his finger at him.

South Wind played in the corner by herself. That shy wind. She worried the windkeeper most of all. South Wind was easily distracted by the silliest of things. A candy wrapper. Angel wings. Why, more than once she even climbed up into God's lap and tickled Him.

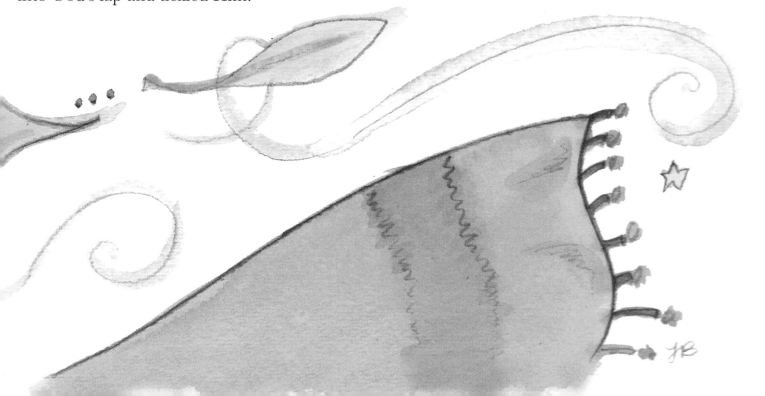

Speaking of the Lord. Wendall sensed His Holy Presence behind him. The windkeeper's belly did a flip. This was it. His Majesty raised His arms. "Come, four winds of heaven. It is time." North Wind rushed to the head of the line. God patiently took him aside. "My warrior wind, full of power and might. You are needed at the end of the line. Your strength will help your brother and sisters reach Earth."

East Wind took her place at the front. This pleased the Lord. "You read my mind, leader wind. Remain humble, yet confident. Your gift of direction will guide your sister and brothers to your destination."

West Wind fluttered God's robe on his way to second in line.

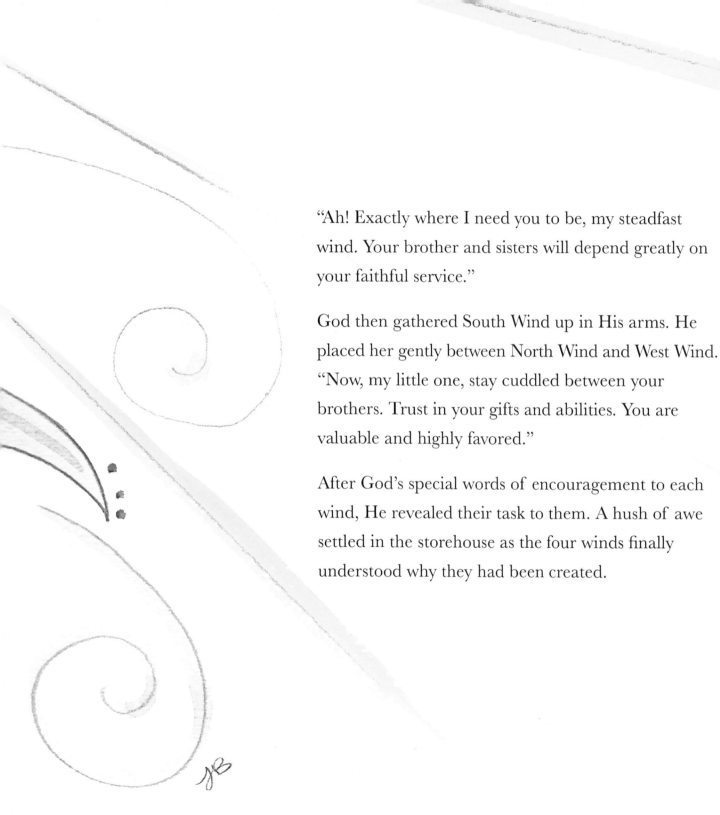

"Ah! Exactly where I need you to be, my steadfast wind. Your brother and sisters will depend greatly on your faithful service."

God then gathered South Wind up in His arms. He placed her gently between North Wind and West Wind. "Now, my little one, stay cuddled between your brothers. Trust in your gifts and abilities. You are valuable and highly favored."

After God's special words of encouragement to each wind, He revealed their task to them. A hush of awe settled in the storehouse as the four winds finally understood why they had been created.

They knew all the stories of old.
How God sent four winds to
breathe life into dry bones.

And when God sent winds over the Earth
to dry the water after the great flood.

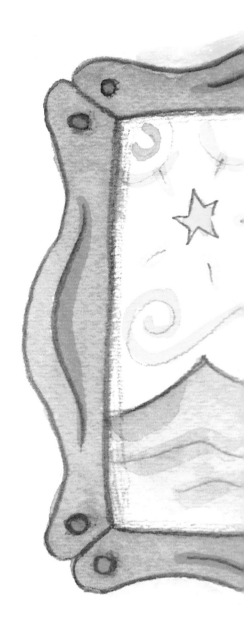

And they'd never forget the story about the wind God used to cause a storm.
Because of that storm, Jonah the prophet was thrown from a ship. God saved him by
sending a big fish to swallow him.

But nothing
in the stories of old compared to this.
The windkeeper bowed his head. Tears wet his cheeks. To be a part of this great plan
filled Wendall with so much love. He worshipped his Lord.

As each grown-up wind passed by the windkeeper, they covered him with loving breezes that dried his tears and ruffled his beard. He lifted his head and blessed each one with a prayer and a smile.

Just as Wendall turned to close the storehouse doors, North Wind sent the windkeeper's cap flying to the ground. That naughty wind. Wendall winked at him.

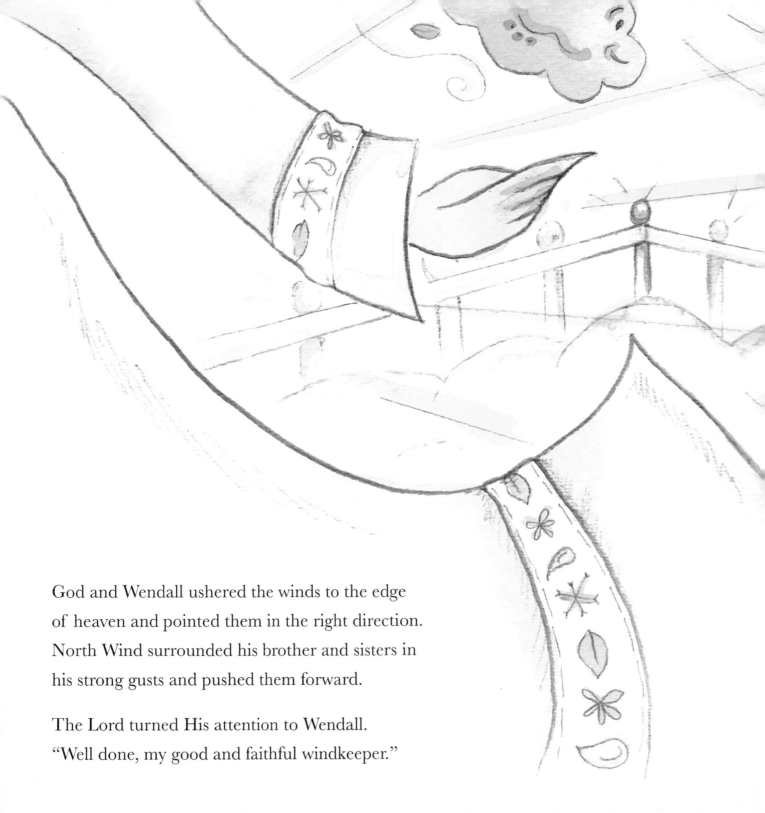

God and Wendall ushered the winds to the edge
of heaven and pointed them in the right direction.
North Wind surrounded his brother and sisters in
his strong gusts and pushed them forward.

The Lord turned His attention to Wendall.
"Well done, my good and faithful windkeeper."

Together they watched those precious winds descend to Earth and move clouds with their gusty breezes. There it was. The star. And it guided three wise men. The four winds worked together as a team. East Wind led her siblings. West Wind remained at their side and kept stray clouds out of the star's path. North Wind offered his strength and power.
And little South Wind tagged along, blowing here and there.

When the wise men reached their destination, Wendall smiled. It filled him with so much joy to witness his Lord's plan unfold. Suddenly, Wendall held his breath. What were those gusty winds up to down there? He saw East Wind, West Wind, and North Wind swirling around the stable. Tears started flowing down his face as he watched his shy little South Wind.

She entered the stable, crawled right up in baby Jesus's lap
and tickled Him. She kissed His cheek and whispered,
"Your Father sends His love."

"[God] makes winds his messengers"
(Psalm 104.4)

Big Words for Little Listeners

Storehouse: *a building where things are stored.*

Gust: *a blast of wind.* The four winds of heaven were gusty, which means they went one direction then another direction real fast like a blast. Gust is also another word for "wind."

Appointed time: *there is a special time to do a specific thing, and it can't be done too early and it can't be done too late. It must be done at just the right time.* In The Windkeeper, God had an appointed time for the four winds of heaven to do their special job. Wendall didn't want them to leave the storehouse too early.

Highly favored: *to honor someone and show them favor.* My daughter has lots of stuffed animals, but there is one bear that she shows favor to, and he has been given the special job night after night of sleeping with her. Her bear is highly favored. In The Windkeeper, the four winds of heaven are highly favored and given the special job of clearing the clouds out of the way so the star can guide the wise men to baby Jesus.

Remain humble, yet confident: *to be sure of yourself and your purpose without being boastful or having an attitude that you are better than someone else.* In The Windkeeper, God encouraged East Wind to be sure of herself but not to think she was better than the other winds. She had to lead her sister and brothers with a humble spirit, knowing that they were a team and she could not do this special job without them.

Steadfast: *to stay strong in something you believe in and don't change your mind or actions.* You stay focused on something and don't give up. The Bible talks about God's love being steadfast. That means God doesn't ever stop loving us. He doesn't change His mind. In The Wind-keeper, God called West Wind His "steadfast wind." Notice that God also used the word "faithful" when talking to West Wind about being steadfast. Faithful is another word for "steadfast."

Awe: *a feeling you get when you experience, see, or hear something incredible or something you've never experienced, seen, or heard before.* Let's face it, God sending Jesus was an incredible plan. In The Windkeeper, the four winds got to be a part of that plan. And they sensed how incredible it was, so a hush of awe settled over the storehouse. They were quiet and filled with wonder as God told them His plan. I bet they even went "Ooh" and "Aah" like we do when we see a new baby, or unwrap a present.

Ruffled: *to mess up something.* Have you ever been outside and the wind messed up your hair? The wind was ruffling your hair. In The Windkeeper, the four winds passed by Wendall and wanted to show him love. How does wind show love? Why, it ruffles your hair (or Wendall's beard).

Ushered: *when someone leads you somewhere.* They show you where to go. In The Windkeeper, God and Wendall showed the four winds where to go.

Before writing The Windkeeper, I researched wind in the Bible

and gained a new understanding to this invisible, yet powerful force that God created. What struck me the most was how God used the wind to accomplish His plans. Some of those plans were revealed in The Windkeeper.

Another example that amazes me was when God sent 10 plagues against Pharaoh because he refused to release God's people from slavery. Exodus 10.13 tells us that God used the east wind to bring a plague of locusts over the land. *"So Moses raised his staff over Egypt, and the Lord caused an east wind to blow over the land all that day and through the night. When morning arrived, the east wind had brought the locusts"* (NLT).

And what happened next is the truly amazing part and something you might not catch unless researching wind. When Pharaoh confessed that he had sinned against the Lord, Moses left his court and pleaded with the Lord. God sent a west wind to drive away the locusts. *"The Lord responded by shifting the wind, and the strong west wind blew the locusts into the Red Sea"* (Exodus 10.19 NLT).

East wind and west wind worked in sync to accomplish God's plans. Truly amazing! My prayer is that The Windkeeper encourages you to open the Bible with your children and read these passages that hold so much power and awesomeness. And a great place to start is with some passages reflected in The Windkeeper:

"Then the LORD sent a great wind on the sea, and such a violent storm arose that the ship threatened to break up" (Jonah 1.4).

This is what the Almighty Lord says: "*Come from the four winds, Breath, and breathe on these people who were killed so that they will live*" (Ezekiel 37.9 GW).

But God remembered Noah and all the wild animals and the livestock that were with him in the ark, and he sent a wind over the earth, and the waters receded (Genesis 8.1).

"*Train a child in the way he should go, and even when he is old he will not turn away from it*" (Proverbs 22.6 GW).

His master replied, "*Well done, good and faithful servant!*" (Matthew 25.21).

The angel went to her and said, "*Greetings, you who are highly favored! The Lord is with you*" (Luke 1.28).

"*For it has pleased the Lord to make you his very own people*" (1 Samuel 12.22 NLT).

"*[God] brings out the wind from his storehouses*" (Psalm 135.7).

"*[God] makes winds his messengers*" (Psalm 104.4).

OTHER PASSAGES ABOUT WIND:
"*He let loose the east wind from the heavens and by his power made the south wind blow*" (Psalm 78.26).

Daniel said: "*In my vision at night I looked, and there before me were the four winds of heaven churning up the great sea*" (Daniel 7.2).

CPSIA information can be obtained
at www.ICGtesting.com
Printed in the USA
BVOW05s1753201017
498245BV00015B/34/P

9 781936 341788